Previewing

Microsoft Office 2000 Professional

Objectives

► **Examine improvements to the installation process**
► **Use personal menus**
► **Use personal toolbars**
► **Learn how to use multiple languages**
► **Explore changes to dialog boxes**
► **Explore changes to switching between open files**
► **Explore changes to other commonly used features**
► **Explore new features of Microsoft Word**
► **Explore new features of Microsoft Excel**
► **Explore new features of Microsoft Access**
► **Explore new features of Microsoft PowerPoint**
► **Examine new online features**

Having learned about Office 97, you are probably curious about Office 2000, the latest version of the Office programs. What are the differences? Why might someone be better off using Office 2000 instead of Office 97? When you hear about new technology, you probably ask yourself questions like these and wonder whether you should upgrade. **Upgrading** is the process of placing a more recent version of a product onto your computer. This unit will introduce you to some of the main differences between Office 97 and Office 2000.

Office

Installing Microsoft Office 2000

Before you can use a software product, you must **install** it on your computer, which involves copying the files from the CDs or floppy disks that make up the software product onto your computer. Most software products will begin the installation process for you when you first insert the CD or floppy disk. Installing Office 2000 will vary according to your computer and network specifics. Be sure to check with your instructor or network administrator before installing any software. The following terms will help take you through the basics of installation.

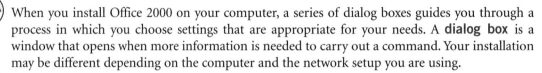

QuickTip

Note that this unit was developed using Office 2000 Professional.
Your Office 2000 may contain different features, depending on the edition you purchased. See Table 1 for a list of the available editions of Office 2000 and what comes with each edition. You might also see differences because this unit was developed using a prerelease version of Office 2000.

When you install Office 2000 on your computer, a series of dialog boxes guides you through a process in which you choose settings that are appropriate for your needs. A **dialog box** is a window that opens when more information is needed to carry out a command. Your installation may be different depending on the computer and the network setup you are using.

As you go through these dialog boxes, you'll notice they usually have default settings selected. **Default settings** are options that the software developer selects as the most commonly used, such as installing the spell checker. You can always select something other than the default settings, but you should become familiar with all the program's features before changing them.

In Office 1997 and Office 2000, one of the default settings is to install only the most popular or commonly used programs and components, such as Word. Additional programs and features are installed only when you try to use them for the first time. In Office 97, once you are using the programs, you can't see what additional features could be installed. However, with Office 2000, commands and buttons for features that are not installed still appear in the program window. When you click those commands and buttons, a dialog box opens, prompting you to insert your installation CD. Inserting your installation CD enables you to install the feature immediately, without requiring you to close any open programs. This option is called **Install on first use**. When you install Office 2000, you can accept the default settings for which features are installed. You can also customize the installation by choosing which features you want to install, which you want to install on first use, or which you would like to become unavailable after installation. See Figure B-1.

Personalization is another big benefit of upgrading to Office 2000. By installing features as needed, you end up with a customized set of programs, containing only the standard Microsoft features and the non-standard features that you choose to install. Furthermore, the "Install on first use" feature saves considerable space on your computer's hard drive by not automatically installing all of the Office features.

FIGURE B-1: Selecting which features to install

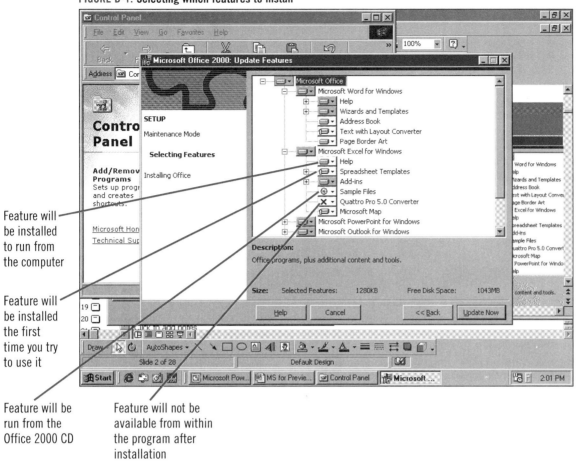

Feature will be installed to run from the computer

Feature will be installed the first time you try to use it

Feature will be run from the Office 2000 CD

Feature will not be available from within the program after installation

TABLE B-1: Editions of Microsoft Office 2000

edition	programs
Standard	Word, Excel, PowerPoint, and Outlook
Small Business	Word, Excel, Outlook, Publisher, and Small Business Tools
Professional	Word, Excel, PowerPoint, Access, Outlook, Publisher, and Small Business Tools
Premium	Professional plus FrontPage and PhotoDraw
Developer	Premium plus tools and documentation for building, managing, and organizing programs

Office

Using Personalized Menus

In each Office program, you can perform tasks using a **menu command** (a word or phrase on a menu that you click to perform a task) or a **toolbar button** (which corresponds to a commonly used menu command). In previous versions of Office, the menus contained and displayed commands for all the installed features. However, as the programs become more powerful, the list of commands gets long and difficult to navigate. For this reason, Microsoft developed "personalized" menus. **Personalized menus** (also referred to as "adaptive," "expanding," "full and short," and "cascading") adapt themselves to fit your work habits. As you work in Office 2000 programs, commands that you use most often are put on the short personal menus. The ones you don't use are hidden, but remain available. You can return your menus to their default settings by resetting your usage data. Resetting usage data erases the record of the commands you have used.

Steps

1. Start Word, click **Insert** on the menu bar to display its short personal menu, compare your screen to Figure B-2

   The commands displayed on your short Insert menu are probably different from those in Figure B-2, which are the default commands. You'll return the menus to their defaults, so the commands you see on your computer will match the figures as you complete these steps.

2. Click **Insert** on the menu bar again to close the menu

3. Click **Tools** on the menu bar, click **Customize** (you might need to pause until the full menu appears to see the command), then click the **Options** tab in the Customize dialog box

4. Make sure the **Menus show recently used commands first** check box and the **Show full menus after a short delay** check box are selected, click the **Reset my usage data** button, click **Yes** to confirm that you want to reset the commands, then click the **Close** button

5. Click **Insert** on the menu bar again, notice that there is no Bookmark command, then pause until the full Insert menu appears, as shown in Figure B-3

   Notice that the commands from the short menu appear on the regular gray background (sometimes referred to as "3D"), and that the commands belonging to the long menu appear on a lighter gray background ("non 3D").

6. Click **Bookmark**

7. Click **Cancel** to close the Bookmark dialog box

8. Click **Insert** on the menu bar to display the short personal menu

   Notice the Bookmark command now appears on the short personal menu because you used it.

9. Click **Insert** on the menu bar again to close the menu

FIGURE B-2: Default short Insert menu

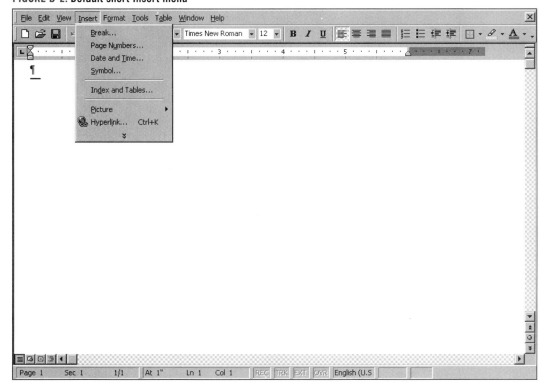

FIGURE B-3: Full Insert menu

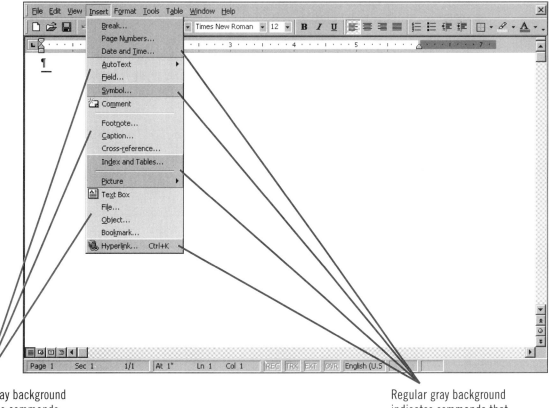

Light gray background
indicates commands
that are not on the
short menu

Regular gray background
indicates commands that
are on the short menu

Office

Using Personalized Toolbars

In each Office program, the **toolbar buttons** (which correspond to commonly used menu commands) are also used frequently to perform common tasks. As with Office menus, the toolbars display the most commonly used buttons for all the installed features. But, with all the features available in Office 2000 (even those that might not yet be installed), the list of buttons can get lengthy, making it difficult to locate the ones you need. To address this problem, Microsoft developed the same "personalized" menu feature for toolbars. **Personalized toolbars** (also referred to as "adaptive," "expanding," and "full and short") adapt themselves to fit your work habits. When you use an Office 2000 program for the first time, the toolbars display only the most commonly used buttons so that there is less clutter in the program window. To display the hidden buttons on a toolbar, click the More Buttons button ⟩. You can also restore personalized toolbars to their default settings by resetting your usage data.

Steps

1. Note that the Standard and Formatting toolbars appear side by side below the menu bar, as shown in Figure B-4

   To learn how you can adjust toolbars to suit your work habits, you'll first set them to make sure they appear on the same row and then you'll reset your usage data so the default buttons are displayed.

2. Click **Tools** on the menu bar, click **Customize**, click the **Options** tab in the Customize dialog box, click the **Standard and Formatting toolbars share one row** check box to select it, as shown in Figure B-4, click the **Reset my usage data** button, click **Yes** to confirm you want to reset the commands, then click **Close**

   Now the Formatting toolbar sits to the right of the Standard toolbar. Notice that you can see some of the Standard toolbar buttons and some of the Formatting toolbar buttons. The rest of the buttons are stored in the More Buttons drop-down list for each toolbar. Your available buttons may be different.

3. Click the **More Buttons button** ⟩ at the right side of the Standard toolbar

   See Figure B-5.

4. Click the **Show/Hide ¶** button ¶

   Notice that the Show/Hide ¶ button moves to the visible part of the Standard toolbar and the Highlight button ✐▾ on the Formatting toolbar disappears (it moved into the Formatting toolbar's More Buttons list). Your buttons may be different.

5. Click ¶ again to return the formatting marks to their original setting

To turn off personalized toolbars

You may find that you like the way the toolbars in Office 2000 change to meet your work habits, or you might prefer to display the toolbars on different rows so that all the buttons are always visible. To display the Standard and Formatting toolbars on separate rows:

1. Click **Tools** on the menu bar, and then click **Customize**.
2. Click the **Options** tab in the Customize dialog box.

3. Click the Standard and Formatting toolbars share one row check box to remove the check mark.
4. Click the **Close** button in the Customize dialog box to close the dialog box.

Similarly, you can turn off the short personal menu by removing the check marks from the Menus show recently used commands first check box and the Show full menus after short delay check box on the Options tab in the Customize dialog box.

FIGURE B-4: Customizing toolbars

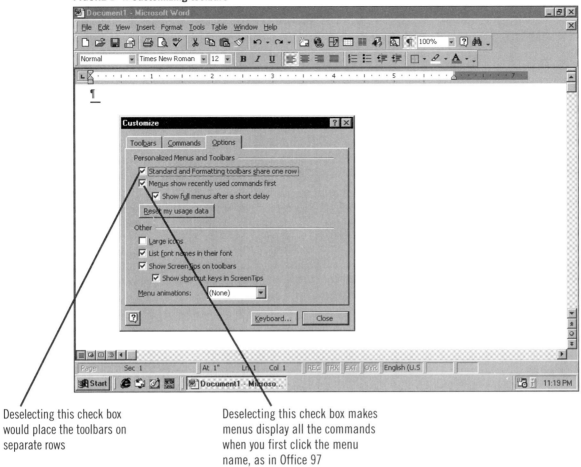

Deselecting this check box would place the toolbars on separate rows

Deselecting this check box makes menus display all the commands when you first click the menu name, as in Office 97

FIGURE B-5: Standard and Formatting toolbars on one row

Standard toolbar

More buttons button for Standard toolbar

Formatting toolbar

Office

Office

Using Multiple Languages in Office 2000

Our global economy means that many companies do business with clients who speak multiple languages. Microsoft created several different versions of Office 97 to support different languages, but each computer can usually be installed with only one language. With Office 2000, you can change the **interface language**, the language used in command names, dialog boxes, Help, and so on. This is because there is only one **code base** (set of programming instructions) and **executable file** (a file that tells a computer how to perform tasks) for each program, rather than multiple executable files of each program for multiple languages. Figure B-6 shows a German interface. No matter what interface language you choose in Office 2000, you can create and edit documents in any language.

Steps 1 2 3 4

1. Click the **Start** button on the taskbar, point to **Programs**, point to **Microsoft Office Tools**, then click **Microsoft Office Language Settings**
   The Microsoft Office Language Setting dialog box opens, as shown in Figure B-7.

2. If necessary, click the **Enabled Languages** tab
   To add a language, click its check box to select it. See Figure B-8.

3. Scroll through the list of languages you can install
   You don't want to install any languages now, so you close the dialog box without making any changes.

4. Click the **Cancel** button

FIGURE B-6: Menus and toolbars in German

Menus and toolbars
after changing
interface language
to German

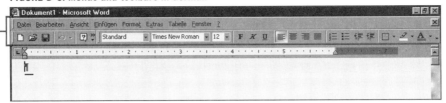

FIGURE B-7: Changing the interface language

Click to change the
interface language

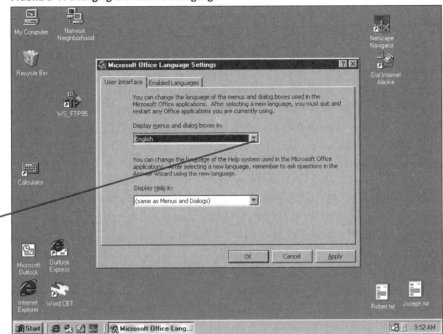

FIGURE B-8: Adding enabled languages

Languages you
can enable, thereby
gaining access to
that language's
dictionary, thesaurus,
and spelling checker

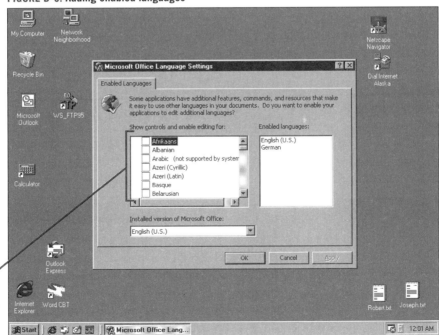

Office

Exploring Changes to Dialog Boxes

In previous versions of Office, commonly used dialog boxes were often awkward to use or unnecessarily complicated to navigate. In Office 2000, Microsoft added features to some of the most often used dialog boxes including the Open, Save, and Save As dialog boxes.

Details

The most obvious dialog box change involves size. In Office 2000, the dialog boxes are bigger, providing more room to display files. This is helpful when you are looking for a certain file and have many files in one location—you can see them all at once rather than having to scroll to see them. See Figures B-9 and B-10 for a comparison of the Open dialog box with the same folder displayed in Excel 97 and Excel 2000.

Second, there is a **Places Bar**, a vertical list of buttons that provides quick access to commonly used folders. See Figure B-10 for a visual representation of the Places Bar and Table B-2, which lists and describes each button found on the Places Bar. In Office 97, you can access the Recent folder, the My Documents folder, the Desktop, and the Favorites folder from these dialog boxes, but it takes several more steps than simply clicking the button on the Places Bar.

A third change to the Open, Save, and Save As dialog boxes is the addition of buttons and commands that make copying, moving, and deleting files right from these dialog boxes much easier. The **Back button** displays the last location you visited, while the new **Delete button** allows you to delete selected files without right-clicking them. The **Search the Web button** starts your browser so that you can find files easily, whether they're located on your computer or on a Web server. See Figure B-10 for the location of these buttons.

TABLE B-2: Places Bar buttons and their functions

button	description
History	Displays the Recent folder, which contains shortcuts to the last 20 locations you visited and files you opened. In Office 97, the Recent list could be only nine files long, it contained shortcuts only to files (not folders or drives), and there was no button to display it easily in the Open, Save, and Save As dialog boxes.
My Documents	Displays the My Documents folder, which is created by Windows and is normally found on the main hard drive of your computer. You can rename and move the folder to make it more useful to you, and those changes will be reflected in the Open, Save, and Save As dialog boxes.
Desktop	Displays the shortcuts found on the Windows desktop. The desktop is actually a folder called Desktop that is created by Windows and is located on your hard drive. Since you can place files and shortcuts to files on the desktop, having quick access to the Desktop folder from the Open, Save, and Save As dialog boxes makes using those files and shortcuts even easier.
Favorites	Displays the items found in the Favorites folder, another folder created by Windows and located on your hard drive. Like the My Documents folder, you can rename and move the Favorites folder to suit your needs, and the changes will be reflected in the Places Bar.
Web Folders	If you have access to a Web server that supports this new feature of Office 2000, you can use this folder to publish files to the Web.

FIGURE B-9: Open dialog box in Excel 97

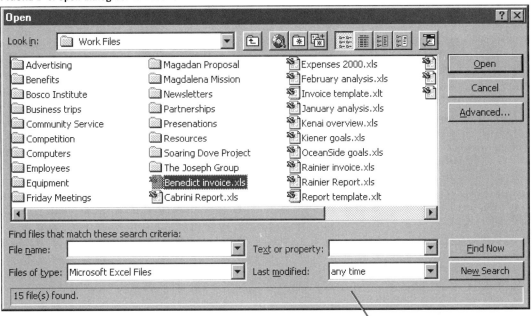

Open dialog box in Excel 97 displaying same folders and files as below; fewer files are visible and there is no Places Bar

FIGURE B-10: Open dialog box in Excel 2000

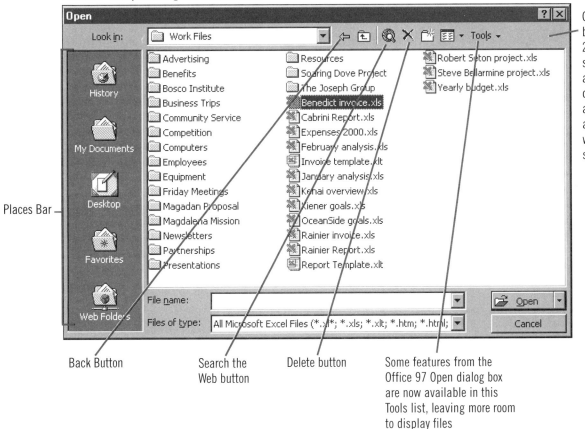

Open dialog box in Excel 2000, with same folders and files displayed as above; all are visible without scrolling

Places Bar

Back Button

Search the Web button

Delete button

Some features from the Office 97 Open dialog box are now available in this Tools list, leaving more room to display files

Office

Exploring Changes to Switching Between Open Files

In previous versions of Office, to switch between two files open in the same program, you click Window on the menu bar, and then click the name of the file you want to switch to. Each open program (not each open file) has a button on the taskbar, so that switching between programs involves a single click, while switching between files takes two or three clicks. In Office 2000, each open file—not just each open program—gets its own button on the taskbar, making it easier to switch between open files created with the same program.

Steps

1. Start Word

2. Type **Microsoft Office 2000** in the new document, then save the file as **Office 2000** on a blank floppy disk

Trouble?

If your taskbar button lists Word first and the filename second, click Tools on the menu bar, click Options, click the View tab if necessary, and then click the Windows in taskbar check box to select it.

3. Open a new, blank document, type **Costs and Benefits of Upgrading**, then save the file to the floppy disk as **Upgrading**

Notice that there are two buttons in the taskbar, one for each file, and that the filename is listed *before* the program name. See Figure B-11.

4. Leave both files open

CLUES TO USE

If you frequently use many files at once, this new quick file switching feature may make your taskbar too cluttered to find the file you need. Regardless of the version of Office you are using, however, it is a good habit to close files you aren't using because it frees up RAM (memory) for the files and programs that you are using.

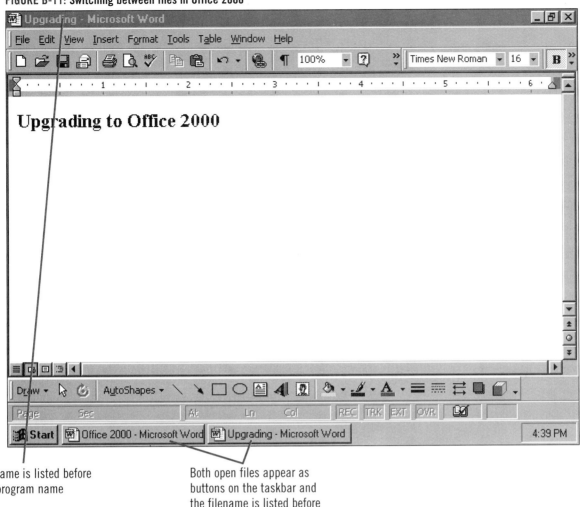

Filename is listed before
the program name

Both open files appear as
buttons on the taskbar and
the filename is listed before
the program name

Exploring Changes to Other Commonly Used Features

In earlier versions of Office, some tasks were unnecessarily complicated or repetitive for the user. Microsoft has responded to this user feedback by creating a powerful new Clipboard and improving the Help system and Clip Gallery.

Details

Using the Office Clipboard

In earlier versions of Office, when you cut or copy data, it is placed on the **Windows Clipboard**, a temporary storage area on your computer's hard drive. The data remains on the Clipboard until you paste it into another location, turn off your computer, or cut or copy other data. In Office 2000, there is also an **Office Clipboard**, a temporary storage area for Office 2000 programs. The Office Clipboard can hold up to 12 selections of data (including data created in other programs and data from the Web), so that you can cut or copy up to 12 different times, without losing your previous selections. You don't have to think about whether your data is placed on the Windows Clipboard or the Office Clipboard, unless your goal is to paste multiple selections into files created with programs other than Office. See Figure B-12.

Getting Help in Office 2000

Like all Microsoft programs, Office 2000 comes with extensive information on how to use the programs. This information, referred to simply as **Help,** is similar to a huge encyclopedia stored on your computer. The **Office Assistant**, an interactive guide to finding information from the Office Help system, is one of the main ways of getting help in both Office 97 and Office 2000. Microsoft changed the Office Assistant in Office 2000 based on user feedback that the Office Assistant be less obtrusive, but remain readily available; that the user be able to turn it off completely while still having access to all the Help information and features; and that it use as much **natural language,** or words and syntax that people use in everyday usage, as possible. Users also requested a Web-like interface and ready access to Help information on the Web. See Figure B-13.

Using the Office 2000 Clip Gallery

Clip art, pictures saved as files for use on a computer, has become an integral part of business documents, personal correspondence, and Web pages. The **Clip Gallery**, a program that organizes pictures, sounds, and motion clips (all of which Microsoft refers to as **clips**), has been improved with Office 2000, making it easier to make your documents more dynamic. In Office 97, inserting a clip into a document involved many steps, after which the Clip Gallery automatically closed. With Office 2000, you can drag clips from the Clip Gallery into your Office documents, placing them at the desired location as you drop them into the document. The Clip Gallery remains open until you close it, making it much easier to insert multiple clips. To facilitate dragging and dropping, the new Clip Gallery window can be resized, minimized, and maximized. Another important improvement in the Office 2000 Clip Gallery is that clips are inserted into documents in their original file formats. See Figure B-14.

FIGURE B-12: Clipboard toolbar

Clipboard toolbar displays icons for up to 12 selections

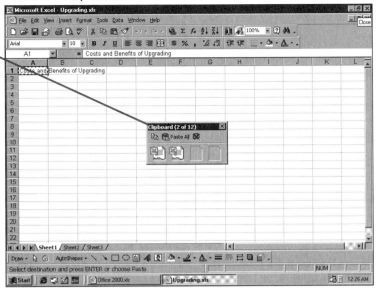

FIGURE B-13: The Office Assistant in Office 2000

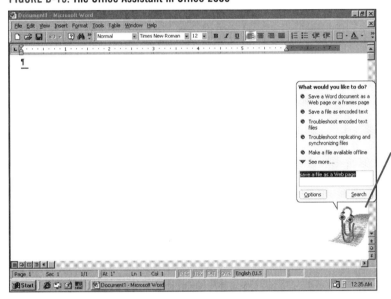

New Office Assistant is smaller, blends into program window better, and presents list of suggested topics in natural language matching the question

FIGURE B-14: Office 2000 Clip Gallery

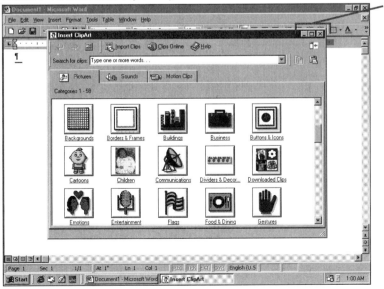

New Clip Gallery can be minimized and resized, unlike the Office 97 Clip Gallery

Office

Examining New Online Features

More companies than ever are advertising on the Web, creating their own Web sites, and using intranets and the Internet to communicate. (**Intranets** are private, company-wide, Web-like connections of computers.) More individuals, too, are using the Web. With Office 2000, all of these tasks become even easier than they were before. Enhanced online capabilities are some of the most powerful and beneficial new features of Office 2000 across applications.

Creating and Editing Web Pages with Office 2000

HTML, or HyperText Markup Language, is the computer programming language used to create and display files for use on the Web. You don't need knowledge of HTML, however, to produce Web pages with Office 97 and Office 2000. Once you save files as HTML (the command in Office 97 is "Save as HTML;" the Office 2000 command is "Save as Web Page"), you can **publish** them to the Web, a process that makes the files available to all who have Internet access. Office 97 files sometimes look different in your Web browser than they do in your Office program. Office 2000 solves this problem by making a cleaner conversion possible. Therefore, when you view Office documents on the Web, the transition is almost seamless—almost no features are lost or distorted.

Publishing Files to the Web with Office 2000

When you publish files, you place them on a **Web server**, a computer connected to the Web that stores files for use on the Web. Most Web servers are maintained by **Internet Service Providers** (ISPs), companies that provide access to the Internet, usually for a fee. With Office 2000, when you create a Web page, a folder is automatically created, using the same name as the Web page file. All the files that are part of the Web page are automatically stored in that folder. Each HTML file you create with Office 2000, therefore, has two easily-managed parts: the HTML file and its corresponding folder. See Figure B-15 and B-16.

Using Online Collaboration in Office 2000

Recent changes in Web technology have made it possible to open a document on one computer and, using an Internet connection and a program such as **Microsoft NetMeeting**, display that document on another computer, so that both computer users can view, edit, and comment on the document. NetMeeting has been available for several years, but is now bundled with Office 2000 Professional. Also, commands have been added to each Office 2000 program that allow you to start NetMeeting right from the Office program and to collaborate with other computer users who have NetMeeting, even if they don't have Office. See Figure B-16.

If both users have microphones attached to their computers, they can discuss the document (and any other topics) using live audio, just like a regular telephone conversation. If both users also have video devices attached to their computers, they can see each other as they talk. If your server uses OSE (Office Server Extensions), you can also use the Online Collaboration command to initiate and join **Web discussions**, a series of comments that users add to Office and HTML documents, making creating documents with other users more efficient.

FIGURE B-15: Automatically created folder for files associated with a Web page, as displayed in Windows Explorer

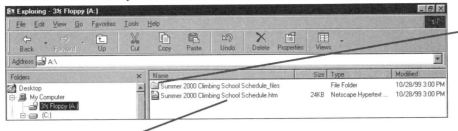

Folder is automatically created (with name to match the Web page) and files associated with the Web page are placed inside

Web page created with Excel 2000

FIGURE B-16: Commands for setting up a NetMeeting conference

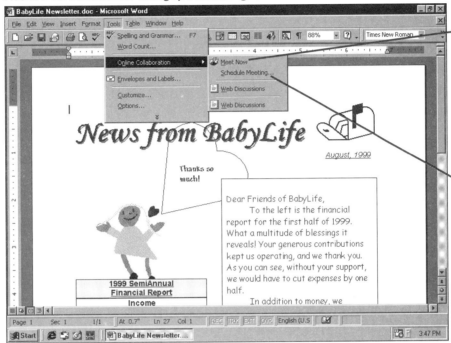

Starts NetMeeting, where you log on to a server and place a call to anyone else running NetMeeting and logged on to that server

Diplays an Outlook e-mail message window where you can select the contact with whom you want to meet and the server you want to use; most of the message is typed for you

CLUES TO USE

Office 2000 Web Folders

If your ISP uses Microsoft's **Office Server Extensions (OSE)**, a set of features and technologies that bridge the gap between Web technology and Office, Windows, and your browser, you can publish files to the Web simply by saving them to your own hard drive or network. This means that you can create, move, delete, and copy HTML files and folders to and from a Web server just as you would to your own hard drive. See Figure B-17. This is possible using a new Office 2000 feature called **Web Folders**, a folder for shortcuts to files on your Web server. The folder is placed on your computer when you install Office 2000.

FIGURE B-17: Adding a Web folder

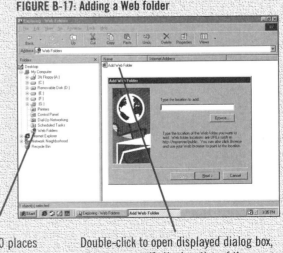

Office 2000 places this new folder on your computer

Double-click to open displayed dialog box, where you specify the location of the server where you want to publish files

Exploring the New Features of Microsoft Word

Office

Microsoft continually tries to improve the overall functionality of how the Office programs work together and individually, and to give each program a wider range of features and greater ease of use. Microsoft Word is the most frequently used of all the office applications. The following is a list of improvements.

Details

Click and Type
In the Print Layout and Web Layout views, you can position the pointer at any blank location in a document and double-click to position the insertion point there (alignment and blank lines are automatically formatted and inserted).

Table improvements
You can insert tables as objects so that you can move and resize them as you do other objects. You can also nest tables, one inside the other, wrap text around them, and divide cells into diagonal halves.

Improved Web authoring tools
Web themes provide consistent formatting and are compatible with FrontPage 2000 (see Figure B-18). Word's rich formatting is not lost when you view Web pages in Internet Explorer 4.0 or higher or in Netscape Navigator, and the Web Page Preview command on the File menu allows you to view a document quickly in your browser.

Improved spelling checker
Not only does Word's spell checker and AutoCorrect feature catch "hte" and change it to "the," but it also corrects more complex typos, such as correcting "sracastic" to "sarcastic."

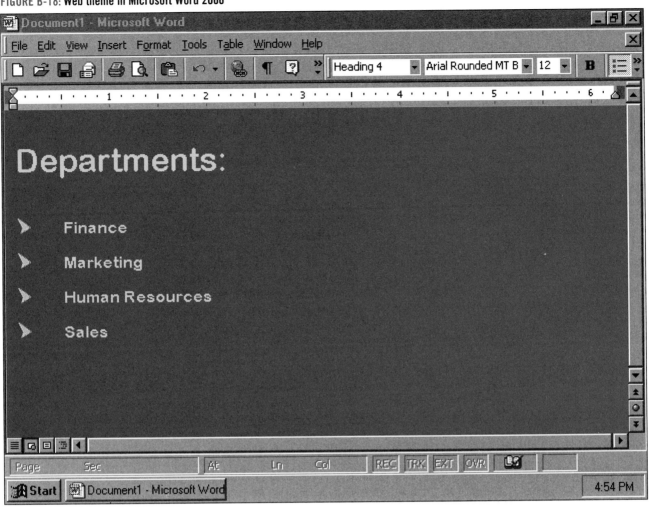

Office

Exploring the New Features of Microsoft Excel

Microsoft continually tries to improve the overall functionality of how the Office programs work together and individually, and to give each program a wider range of features and greater ease of use. Microsoft Excel is the spreadsheet component of the Office applications. The following is a list of improvements.

Details

 ### Built-in HTML file format for Web pages

This feature, available in all Office programs and discussed earlier ("Exploring New Online Features"), represents an especially significant improvement in Excel. In Office 2000, when you save workbooks as HTML, they retain much more formatting, and you have the option of saving it for viewing only from the browser, or saving it as an interactive Web page (allowing Web users to change cells, charts, or PivotTables).

 ### Improved PivotTables and charts

You can link a chart to a PivotTable so it will change automatically when you change the PivotTable. You can also work with a pivot chart directly to move fields, create new ones, and more. You can easily format PivotTables by choosing from a dozen preset formats. See Figure B-19.

 ### Support for the new euro currency

You can display, enter, format and print the euro symbol € and work with values in the euro currency. To type the euro symbol, turn on NumLock, then press Alt+0128.

 ### Browser Copy and Paste

You can drag table data from an Internet Explorer browser window directly into a spreadsheet, and it will be formatted appropriately.

FIGURE B-19: Pivot Table from a preset format

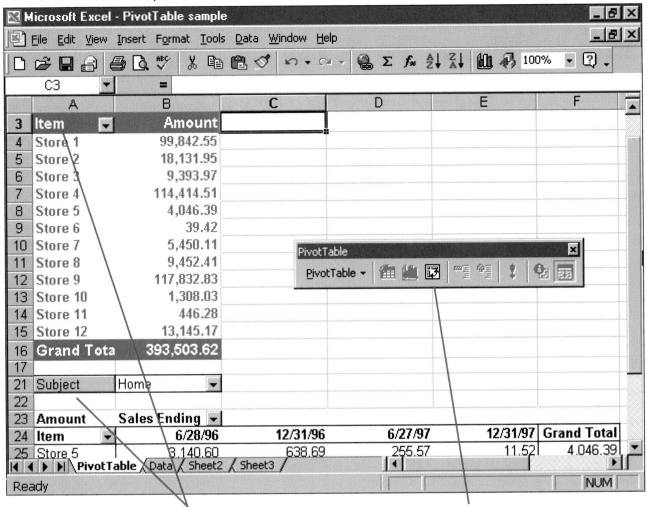

Pivot table buttons that contains
the name of a summarized field
of data

Pivot table toolbar

Office

Exploring the New Features of Microsoft Access

Microsoft continually tries to improve the overall functionality of how the Office programs work together and individually, and to give each program a wider range of features and greater ease of use. Microsoft Access is the database component of the Office applications. The following is a list of improvements.

Details

Name AutoCorrect
Automatically tracks and updates changes to the names of database objects. This feature is extremely useful in keeping all data up to date and accurate, especially in a large, complicated database.

Conditional formatting
Enables you to specify formatting features that appear only when certain conditions are met (for example, the records of all clients from Colorado could be shaded green).

Subdatasheets
Enables you to view and edit related records in tables, queries, or forms from Datasheet view, Query Datasheet view, or Form view. See Figure B-20.

Data access pages
Enables you to create Web pages in Access to collect data over the Web for an Access or SQL server database.

FIGURE B-20: Subdatasheet in Access 2000

CourseID	Description	Hours	MOUS	Prereq	Cost
⊞ Access1	Introduction to Access	12	Proficient	Comp1	$200
⊞ Access2	Intermediate Access	24	Expert	Access1	$400
⊞ AccessLab	Access Case Problems	12		Access2	$200
⊟ Comp1	Computer Fundamentals	12			$200

	LogNo	SSN	Attended	Passed
	1	115-77-4444	01/31/2000	☑
	2	134-70-3883	01/31/2000	☑
∗	(AutoNumber)			☐

CourseID	Description	Hours	MOUS	Prereq	Cost
⊞ Excel1	Introduction to Excel	12	Proficient	Comp1	$200
⊞ Excel2	Intermediate Excel	12	Expert	Excel1	$200
⊞ ExcelLab	Excel Case Problems	12		Excel2	$200

Office

Exploring the New Features of Microsoft PowerPoint

Microsoft continually tries to improve the overall functionality of how the Office programs work together and individually and to give each program a wider range of features and greater ease of use. Microsoft PowerPoint is the presentation component of the Office applications. The following is a list of improvements.

Details

Normal view displays three panes
Normal view displays the current slide, its speaker notes, and an outline of the entire presentation all in the same window, enabling you to work on all aspects of a presentation without switching views. See Figure B-21.

ScreenSaver can be disabled during a slide show
To prevent slide show interruptions, the ScreenSaver is automatically disabled—even if there is no mouse or keyboard activity for long periods of time.

Improved Web authoring
Slide shows lose no formatting when displayed in Internet Explorer 4.0 or above.

FIGURE B-21: Normal view with three panes

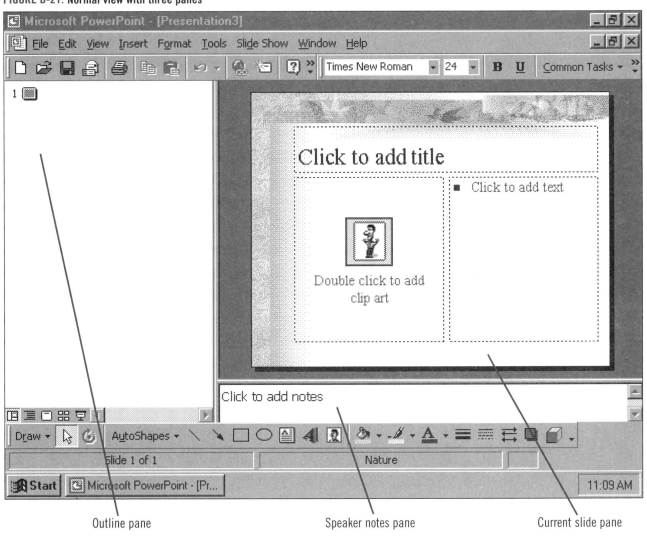

Outline pane   Speaker notes pane   Current slide pane

Preparing
for the Year 2000 Computer Problem

Objectives

► **Understand and assess the Year 2000 computer problem on a PC**

► **Examine how Office 2000 handles the Year 2000 computer problem**

By now you have probably heard much about the Year 2000 computer problem, sometimes referred to as the "millennium bug" or the "Y2K bug" (the Y stands for "year" and the K is an abbreviation for "kilo," a prefix that means "thousand"). The phrase **Year 2000 computer problem** is a catchall term to describe a host of computer difficulties anticipated to occur when we begin the year 2000. This appendix will introduce you to the basics of the Year 2000 computer problem and the steps you can take to protect your own personal computer. In addition, this appendix will examine how the Y2K bug affects Microsoft Office 2000.

Office 2000

Understanding and Assessing the Year 2000 Computer Problem on a PC

The Year 2000 problem is important because computers affect nearly every aspect of most peoples' lives. There are millions of computers in the world, and billions of **embedded control systems**, which are computers (or electronics devices that function like computers) found inside other products. ECSs can be as small as a chip in a watch or as large as a mainframe computer in an electric plant. Every computer and ECS that we want to ensure works through the turn of the millennium needs to be found, tested, and fixed. The information that follows will help you understand how the Year 2000 computer problem affects our lives and help you prepare your personal computer for the turn of the millennium.

Details

Understanding the Year 2000 Computer Problem

The source of the problem goes back to the 1960s, when software was first being used on a widespread basis and the standards for our current software were developed. Software developers who used two digits in their programs saved companies hundreds of thousands of dollars in memory and hard disk space, both of which were significantly more expensive then than they are now. In the years that followed, hardware prices were slow to drop in relation to other costs, so using two-digit years became standard for the first 20-30 years of the computer era. And because new programs have to be compatible with the old—it is often easier and less expensive to extend, patch, and improve upon old software than it is to buy new—the two-digit standard stuck. There may be two, five, ten, or more components of your computer that are involved in producing accurate time and date results. This means that you may have a difficult time determining exactly what in the computer needs to be fixed. You should not, for example, merely set the date to January 1, 2000 and see what happens; you may lose valuable data, and you won't find the source of the problem. Table AP-1 lists and describes the various parts of a computer that use date and time functions.

TABLE AP-1: **Computer components involved in tracking date and time**

Component	Function
The system clock, or **RTC** (Real Time Clock)	An internal clock on the CMOS (see below) that keeps track of time even when the computer is off. Most RTCs have room for only two digits for the century (80 for 1980, for example), so that the year 2000 (00) may be interpreted as 1900.
CMOS, or Complementary Metal Oxide Semiconductor	The memory chip that contains the RTC. The CMOS chip requires only a trickle of current to maintain its settings, supplied by an onboard battery. The CMOS chip stores the settings unique to each computer, such as the time and date, the hard disk type, and BIOS preferences.
The **BIOS** (Basic Input/Output System)	A small program built into computers that starts when a computer is turned on and that relays information between the hardware and the software
The **operating system**	The program that communicates with the BIOS and runs all the other programs, coordinating the interaction and sharing of a computer's components so that they don't interfere with one another
Programs (also called software or applications)	The lists of instructions that tells a computer how to perform various tasks
Data files	Information a user enters and saves on a computer

Assessing and Fixing Year 2000 Problems on a Personal Computer

The problem is made more complex by the fact that a computer has three main components—hardware, software, and data files—and faulty date references in any one of those can cause a computer to produce inaccurate results or to cease to work entirely. For this reason, you should test your personal computer to see whether it will handle the change to the year 2000 correctly. A personal computer represents a significant investment for most people, and many of us are incredibly dependent on them for communication, record-keeping, and working at home. Tests have revealed that even computers made by the same manufacturer and running the same software will respond to the change to 2000 differently. So even if your computer hardware and/or software vendors claim that their products are free of year 2000 problems, you would be wise to perform a few tests yourself and assess your data files and how you entered dates.

The general steps you should take to get your computer ready for the year 2000 are as follows:

- Back up your data files and make sure you have installation disks for all of your software, including device drivers (software for peripheral devices), and a system disk.

- List the components of your computer that you need to assess (include the processor, the BIOS, hard disks, disk drives, the modem, printers, and fax, as well as your operating system and software programs). List the manufacturer and model names, serial numbers, and other pertinent data (such as processor speed, hard disk capacity, and program versions). You may have to refer to this list if your computer malfunctions after December 31 or while you are performing tests.

- Test each component for year 2000 compliance. The best way to do this is to run a program designed to test various computer components for problems with the year 2000. Many such programs exist, and many, many more are likely to be developed in the middle and later parts of 1999. You can either get such a program free from the Internet or spend between $20 and $40 for one. See Table AP-2.

- Formulate and implement a solution for each component that handles the year 2000 incorrectly. You might need to install a **patch** (an update to a program) that the vendor creates (these are often available on the Web), or you might need to purchase and install new hardware and/or software components. You might also need to re-enter the four-digit dates in all of your data files and enter all new dates with four digits. Note that you will probably have multiple solutions—one for each component that mishandles the year 2000.

- Re-test each component.

The testing and fixing process can be complicated, and it will be different for each computer. You can also find hundreds of books, articles, and Web sites devoted to the topic. See Table AP-2 for a brief list.

Note: You should contact your computer's vendor for information specific to your computer system before you perform any tests.

Office 2000

TABLE AP-2: **Resources for assessing and fixing year 2000 problems in a personal computer**

URL or book title	Web site creator or book publisher	Description
www.microsoft.com/y2k	Microsoft	Includes a guide to all Microsoft products, a list of frequently asked questions, and compliancy definitions
www.support2000.com	Support2000	Offers help to small business owners who are just getting started on their year 2000 planning.
Know2000	The Year 2000 Group, Inc.	A program that takes you through the process of checking your hardware and software, then prepares a summary and a suggested plan of action. Includes a database of Y2K-readiness reports for more than 3,500 home and small business programs, and a database of hardware vendors.
Norton 2000	Symantec	A program that tests your hardware, software, and data files. It is especially helpful for Excel users, because it analyzes Excel workbooks, makes copies of them, then color-codes and annotates each cell (in the copied files, leaving the originals as they were) to help you find and fix year 2000 problems.
Check 2000 PC	Greenwich Mean Time (1-800-216-5545)	A program that tests and fixes BIOS problems, then tells you which programs and data will be affected by the year 2000. Also helps you prioritize fixing any problems it finds on your PC.
www.y2k.policyworks.gov	U.S. Federal Government	A comprehensive list of vendors and their products, which you can search to determine year 2000 compliance.

Office 2000 and the Year 2000

As you develop your strategy for making sure your computer will work in the next millennium, one component you may decide to upgrade is your programs. The Office 2000 suite of programs is deemed "Year 2000 Compliant," a feature that may save you considerable time, money, and effort. **Y2K compliant** is a term applied to various computer products; it describes a product that the manufacturer says will handle the year 2000 appropriately. However, there is no industry standard that defines "Y2K compliant;" nor is there any regulation that ensures products claiming to be compliant are using the term accurately and consistently. An important benefit of Office 2000 is that it also has new features to help prevent problems caused by the year changing to 2000. Office 2000 has been labeled Y2K compliant by Microsoft, meaning that if the other components in your computer are also compliant, dates will be handled correctly before and after 2000.

 To eliminate confusion about its own products, Microsoft created a strategy containing a statement defining what it means when it calls one of its products "Y2K compliant." They have also created a list of products that are Y2K compliant, those that need patches or service packs in order to become compliant, those that are not compliant, those that have not yet been assessed, and those that will not be tested for compliance. You can read this statement (along with its lengthy disclaimer) and access the list of products and their compliance levels at *http://www.microsoft.com/technet/year2k/*. The site also has general Year 2000 information and links to Web sites that give or sell programs to test your computer.

 Both Office 2000 and Office 97 use 2029 as the pivot year, so if you haven't encountered any problems working in Office 97, you don't have to change any settings when you upgrade to Office 2000. Note that changing the pivot year has nothing to do with what dates you can enter and expect Office 2000 to use accurately. The **pivot year** refers only to the 100-year period for which you can use two-digit dates. You can enter any year you want using four digits. See Figure AP-1.

FIGURE AP-1: Changing the two-digit pivot year

Click up or down list arrow to change pivot year

Now that you've had a chance to explore the new features of Office 2000, you can assess the advantages of upgrading and balance those with your computer needs and your budget. If you do decide to upgrade, you can use this appendix as a resource, along with the powerful Office Help system, to learn how to use the new features, minimizing the time you spend learning and maximizing the time you spend actually using the new features to create effective documents for work and pleasure.

Resources

http://www.microsoft.com/technet/year2k/

http://www.microsoft.com/office/preview/

http://www.cnn.com/TECH/specials/y2k/

JD Consulting: *Year 2000 Personal Computer Fix-It Guide*. Charles River Media, Rockland, MA, 1999.

Yourdon, Edward, and Jennifer Yourdon: *Time Bomb 2000: Revised and Updated*. Prentice Hall, Upper Saddle River, NJ, 1999.

Webster, Bruce. *The Y2K Survival Guide: Getting to, Getting through, and Getting Past the Year 2000 Problem*. Prentice Hall, Upper Saddle River, NJ, 1999.

Index